When Grandma Gatewood Took a Hike

To M. G. W.

— Michelle Houts

For all children young and old who love our Earth,
most especially Nina and Sophia.

— Erica Magnus

When Grandma Gatewood Took a Hike

Written by Michelle Houts

Illustrated by Erica Magnus

Many years ago in a not-so-fancy, rather crowded log house in the woods not far from the Ohio River, Emma Rowena Caldwell Gatewood grew up with fourteen brothers and sisters. Eventually, she got married and raised eleven children of her own.

Emma had the greenest thumb and the most bountiful garden north of the Ohio River. She relished life's simple joys, like finding Dutchman's-breeches in bloom on a spring morning and visiting with neighbors near and far.

When other folks started to buy cars, Emma chose to walk. She walked over a hill to care for an ailing neighbor. She walked to town to clean houses for others. Five minutes or five miles, Emma didn't mind the walk.

The roads of Appalachia twisted and turned, but Emma's route always took the most direct path—as the crow flies. No matter that it took a body over hills, through thickets, or across streams, Emma always got where she was going on foot.

One day, after her children were grown and raising children of their own, Emma picked up a magazine. She found a story about a man who had spent months walking the entire length of the Appalachian Trail. It was a long hike. Two thousand miles long between Georgia and Maine. Several men had completed the journey, but not one woman.

"Hmmph," thought spunky old Emma. "If a man can do it, so can I!"

Of course, Emma was an experienced walker. But hiking? Hiking was not something she knew much about. So, she read about what she might need on the trail, and she sewed a nifty sack from a yard of denim fabric. She stuffed it full of clothing and food.

Then, on a morning in July, Emma Gatewood went by bus to Maine and climbed up Mount Katahdin. After she signed her name on the official Appalachian Trail register, she was on her way! If she walked south and stayed on the trail, she'd be in Georgia before Thanksgiving.

On the first day, she hiked over rocks and around a lake. She saw blueberry bushes and chipmunks, but very few hikers. This didn't bother Emma. She liked being on her own in the middle of nature.

But her aloneness didn't last long. As she passed by a rain-rotted sign on the trail, a swarm of blackflies decided to join her. Pesky and bitey, the blackflies wouldn't leave. Emma swatted and batted at them until she noticed the trail was not much of a trail anymore. She wandered for hours.

She was lost.

Emma Gatewood didn't get discouraged. She built a fire and stayed put. Throughout the night, cold rain fell as she tried to sleep on the hard ground. The next morning, she set out again. Once, she lost her eyeglasses. She couldn't find them anywhere and then . . .

Crunch!

Without her glasses, Emma was doomed. She tried to fix them with a Band-Aid, but that didn't work out so well.

Overhead, two airplanes buzzed the treetops. They flew low and slow.

"Now what in the world could they be looking for?" Emma wondered. Then it hit her like an acorn falling from an oak tree. They were searching for her!

The search planes couldn't see the tiny old lady lost in the brush. So, she decided to hike back the way she had come. When she rounded a bend and ran smack dab into a search party, everyone was surprised.

A park ranger took one look at Emma Gatewood, with her fly bites and broken glasses, and shook his head.

"Go home, Grandma," he told her.

He was the first person (besides her own grandchildren) to call Emma Rowena Caldwell Gatewood "Grandma." But he surely wouldn't be the last.

Just like that, Grandma Gatewood's dream of hiking the Appalachian Trail had ended. Back to Ohio she went.

As summer turned to fall, Grandma Gatewood continued to do all the things she loved. She visited family in California. Back home in Ohio, she taught her grandchildren to recognize the calls of birds in the meadows. On walks in the woods, she pointed out tiny bluets that grew in the cool shade and lingered well into July.

When her late-summer garden was overflowing, Grandma took to canning. She put up jellies and jams, pickles, and wax beans. Her cupboards were bursting with the fruit of her hard work.

And when fall turned to winter, Grandma cared for folks who were sick. She quilted and sewed and scribbled down poems as they popped into her head.

But all through the seasons, the Appalachian Trail was never far from Grandma Gatewood's thoughts. She just had to find a way to fulfill her dream.

Then one day, she had a thought.

"If I can't walk the trail from north to south, I'll walk it from south to north!"

So out came the denim bag again, but this time Grandma packed very little. A baby bottle for water, a plastic shower curtain for a tent, a change of clothing, a light blanket, and a little bit of food. She didn't own a pair of hiking boots. High-top sneakers suited Grandma just fine.

On a chilly day in early May, Grandma Gatewood stood atop Mount Oglethorpe in Georgia. She signed the Appalachian Trail register and started walking north.

As Grandma hiked, she made friends with other hikers. She didn't mind sharing the trail, but she wasn't too pleased whenever a hiker went around her.

When the trail crossed meadows and farms, Grandma met families who offered her food or invited her to sleep in their house or barn. Other times the trail crossed mountains, and Grandma was all alone. She ate from the wilderness. Growing up in the hills of Ohio had been good training for finding edible plants and natural springs. After walking many miles every day, Grandma Gatewood had no trouble sleeping at night, even on the cold, rocky ground. And this time, she kept her eyeglasses safely tucked away.

When Grandma Gatewood came across snakes, she carefully walked around them.

When the bitey blackflies joined her again,
she made a hat of sassafras leaves and the
tiny pests left her alone.

Once, while Grandma was enjoying a tin of sardines, a bobcat lingered nearby, making loud, hungry noises.

"If you come too close, I'll crack you," Grandma called out to the bobcat. He never came any closer.

Pretty soon Grandma's journey became the talk of the nation. Magazine and newspaper reporters told her story as she hiked. She wasn't terribly fond of having her picture taken, but every now and then she'd pause for a photographer along the way. The whole country was cheering for the little old grandmother from Ohio.

Finally, on a cold, gray day in late September, Emma Rowena Caldwell Gatewood reached the top of Mount Katahdin in Maine, finishing the journey she had started almost five months earlier. When she set her pack down, she broke into song. Her joyous strains of "America the Beautiful" echoed down the mountain and along the trail, announcing the arrival of the most-loved hiker in America.

Her words of accomplishment offered inspiration to all who would follow her example.

"I did it. I said I'd do it, and I've done it!"

Grandma Hiked On

In 1955, at age sixty-seven, Emma Gatewood became the first woman to successfully solo hike the Appalachian Trail in one continuous journey. Once she got a taste for the trail, there was no stopping her. Less than two years later she repeated her amazing journey. No one, man or woman, had ever accomplished this feat twice. Grandma had set another record! A person would think twice was enough, but Grandma Gatewood ended up walking the Appalachian Trail a third time. This time, she did it in sections.

By then, most folks expected Grandma Gatewood to trade in her high-top sneakers for a pair of cozy slippers, but she still had a hankering for hiking. She heard about a wagon train leaving Independence, Missouri, and traveling all the way to Oregon City, Oregon, along what was once the Oregon Trail to celebrate the hundredth anniversary of the first pioneers' journey. This exciting new adventure was more than Grandma could resist.

So, just like the pioneers one hundred years before, Grandma Gatewood headed west. When she got to the starting point, she was surprised to learn that the wagon train had already left. Without another thought, she headed out on her own by foot. The two-thousand-mile walk made her even more famous. She arrived in Oregon City two weeks before the wagon train that inspired her hike!

After that, Grandma hiked mostly in Ohio. She cleaned up a trail near her Gallia County home. Every year, she led hikers through one of her favorite sections of the Buckeye Trail in the Hocking Hills.

Today, hikers who follow Grandma's favorite trail from Old Man's Cave to Ash Cave in the Hocking Hills are walking on the Grandma Gatewood Trail, named in loving memory of Emma Gatewood. If you walk the Grandma Gatewood Trail, and if you take your time and look around, you will see the same rocks and trees that inspired Grandma Gatewood. You will hear the rush of the water pouring over Cedar Falls, just as when Grandma walked the very same path.

And, just maybe, you will think of Grandma Gatewood as you set your sights on your own goals. No matter what mountains might stand in your way.

Grandma Gatewood with Anne and Elizabeth Bell at Sugarloaf
Mountain, Maine, in 1955. *Photo by Richard H. Bell.*

Source Notes

I came across many books, articles, interviews, people, and places while researching Grandma Gatewood's first attempts to hike the Appalachian Trail. Those used in creating this book were *Hiking the Appalachian Trail, Volume One,* edited by James R. Hare; *Grandma Gatewood Walks across America,* by Lillian Gatewood Sullivan; *Grandma Gatewood's Walk,* by Ben Montgomery; "A Touch of Sassafras," from *Ohio Bell Perspective,* September 12, 1969; "Mrs. Emma Gatewood," from *Sports Illustrated,* August 15, 1955; "Pioneer Grandmother," from *Sports Illustrated,* October 10, 1955; and "Armed with Determination," by Merrill C. Gilfillan, from the *Columbus Dispatch Magazine,* November 1, 1964. Videos produced by Eden Valley Enterprises offered stories from Emma's children and grandchildren. The Gallia County Historical Society houses many helpful articles and artifacts from Grandma Gatewood's hikes. Marjorie Wood, Emma's great-granddaughter, was also a source of many stories, photographs, articles, and artifacts.

Ohio University Press, Athens, Ohio 45701 • www.ohioswallow.com

© 2016 by Michelle Houts. All rights reserved

To obtain permission to quote, reprint, or otherwise reproduce or distribute material from Ohio University Press publications, please contact our rights and permissions department at (740) 593-1154 or (740) 593-4536 (fax). Printed in the United States of America. Ohio University Press books are printed on acid-free paper ⊚ ™

Printed in Canada.

21 20 19 18   5 4 3

Library of Congress Cataloging-in-Publication Data
Names: Houts, Michelle. | Magnus, Erica, illustrator.
Title: When Grandma Gatewood took a hike / written by Michelle Houts ; illustrated by Erica Magnus.
Description: Athens, Ohio : Ohio University Press, [2016] | Includes bibliographical references. | Audience: Ages: 4–8.
Identifiers: LCCN 2016019900 | ISBN 9780821422359 (hc : acid-free paper) | ISBN 9780821445808 (pdf)
Subjects: LCSH: Gatewood, Emma Rowena Caldwell, 1887–1973—Juvenile literature. | Hikers—Appalachian Trail—Biography—Juvenile literature. | Women conservationists—Appalachian Trail—Biography—Juvenile literature. | Appalachian Trail—History—Juvenile literature.
Classification: LCC GV199.92.G35 H68 2016 | DDC 796.51092 [B] —dc23
LC record available at https://lccn.loc.gov/2016019900